# please don't buy me
# me
# ice cream

## a child's rules for priceless parenting

# Dana M. Greco

**Outskirts Press, Inc.**
**Denver, Colorado**

Outskirts Press, Inc.
http://www.outskirtspress.com

ISBN: 978-1-4327-2771-0

Outskirts Press and the "OP" logo are trademarks belonging to Outskirts Press, Inc.

PRINTED IN THE UNITED STATES OF AMERICA

*I dedicate this book to my two daughters, Dixon and Gracie. You both continue to teach me how to parent and enjoy the process.*

# Introduction

There I was during the quiet midnight hours of my first child's birth at an east side hospital in New York City, long after the 12 hours of labor, the screaming, the rhythmic breathing and joys and terrors that go along with the anticipation, the prenatal appointments, the ultrasounds, the birthing classes, the elastic stretch maternity clothes, the swollen ankles, the indigestion... you know the rest. I was utterly exhausted. I fell asleep. Not knowing then that this would be my last deep sleep for many years... a nurse nudged me and said, excuse me....Ms....Ms...your baby needs to be fed." Uh?... and I rolled over away from her. "Ms... your baby.... she's hungry...do you need help with her latching on?" Latching on...huh, what is she *talking* about? Still fighting to stay asleep ignoring this intruder... slowly I became conscious ...huh?...oh...wait...I had a baby! I'm a mother, a mommy, me?... a mama?

I perched myself up and cradled her in my arms, this new little human being, this squirmy little sausage in a blanket. I looked into her round blurry eyes and I made a vow to her that I would try to learn everything to the best of my ability of what it means to be a good parent, a great parent. I promised her that I would always be open to suggestions and any advice, and that no matter what, there will always be something to be gained by discovering more. We fell back asleep.

We hear from our own parents, in laws, aunts, uncles, friends, teachers, seasoned and wise women and men who have crossed that bridge, those who have taught us through books, stories and poems of what a parent's role is. Instructed by thoughtful advisors who want to ease our anxiety telling us that all we need to do is our very best. That all children really need is love, and with enough of it they will flourish and thrive. They tell us there are no instruction booklets but with good instincts and nurturing, children will get what they need, and our jobs as parents should not be so complicated. But there *are* instruction booklets for EVERYTHING. Why should there not be one on parenting, right next to the one for the blender, the self-cleaning oven, the remote control and the shampoo... although... just maybe the instructions lie within the hearts of our children.

## **Message from Gracie,
age 13**


One day, a long time from now, I would love to be a parent and have kids of my own. I would raise them in a way that they would grow up to be happy, healthy and successful people. I have given this some thought...As a kid I believe that parenting when appropriate can be taught from their children. I know this book will help many parents because what makes this book unique and helpful is that it is written from a child's point of view. Parents get so caught up in their own stuff. The reader should know the rules in this book were collected by asking many different children from many different families what they needed from their parents and what they thought would help make them grow up to be secure, and joyful people. I hope this book will make parenting a lot easier and a lot more rewarding for all of us.

Let's begin with RULE # 1

**please** don't spoil me. i know very well that i can not have everything i ask for. i'm only testing you.

Chances are you will never hear these words come out of your child's mouth, but it is very possible they may feel this way. Read it again. It is the "I'm only testing you" that speaks to the heart of the matter. What they are testing is "who is in charge?" Who's the ringmaster of this circus?

Children do not want the power and responsibility of having everything for which they ask. As parents, we somehow think it is better for our children to have the things we did not have. To have the life we really deserved. Although that may be true, it is not an excuse for indulging a child.

When a child attempts to negotiate and manipulate to the point of the parent caving in, then we have leadership betrayal. Setting limits makes them feel more secure. Security and structure is a basic need. It is a declaration that parents are in control. Children feel more secure when they know someone else is in charge.

It is difficult for parents to stay firm when a child is whining and pleading, and the justifications to give in are ringing through your head. But ultimately, as parents it is our responsibility to tolerate that unbearable plea, and develop mental and emotional muscle for their sake and ours.

**please** don't let me form bad habits. i rely on
you to detect them in the early stages.

A child needs to be supervised and then directed, then supervised some more and then praised. Handled in a loving and caring manner will be effective and permanent throughout their lives as well as passed down to the next generation. Bad habits can mean not washing their hands before sitting down to dinner, to constantly being disorganized and late for school. It is important for the parent to pay attention to the daily activities that children develop. Get to know who your child is, be observant of their personal behavior and choices. They will be out of the house and in the world faster than you think. Their ability to live independently has everything to do with what they learn as children.

Every parent is a role model. So be aware of the good and bad habits you may have. Try to correct them while instilling good habits in your children. If questionable behavior is detected early enough, the child will not have the added burden of trying to break the cycle of destructive or negative behavior in life. Good habits are a reflection of the values utilized within the family.

**please** don't forget to take me to the park
and playground. it is through my peers that i
learn how to socialize.

Children will watch other children play and by this observation most likely comes a desire to belong. Children will find their way to a group or individual child and begin play. This is their form of communication. When parents "hover" and interfere beyond necessity, it interrupts this development. As hard as it is, as long as your child is not in danger or involved in a group of negative behavior try not to make too much eye contact. Allow your child to navigate their way through social situations. It will strengthen their coping skills which they will need later when you can not be there, because they have outgrown the playground and are in a school yard or better yet an office party.

**please** don't be afraid to be clear and firm with me. i prefer it. it makes me feel secure.

If a parent cannot be clear and firm with the child, then possibly the parent is not comfortable with the role of authority. As a parent it is our responsibility to have the authority. We need to learn how best to utilize this power. Find out for yourself why that might be difficult for you. Begin to ask yourself questions like who was the authority in my family growing up? How did that effect me?

A child needs to know the rules. Employees go to work and expect that there are going to be guidelines, a job description, tasks and expectations of their performance. If the job description is not clear, an employee might find this unsettling, perhaps anxiety provoking. Children have jobs too, to be children to grow and develop and be free in their curiosity. Guidelines and authority figures help the child to accomplish their goals. When a parent can be clear and firm, the child will learn to be respectful and similarly express herself or himself clearly.

Both child and parent can better enjoy the relationship because both feel secure in their respective positions.

**please** don't wait until i get to kindergarten
before you prepare me for my education.

Children are like sponges. They absorb the world around them. Education is everywhere and can be accessible at all times. Preparing your child for the strategies of learning can begin from the stroller. Use words like homework at home before they begin school, so that when they get to school it is not a foreign word, or a scary word, but rather a pleasant past time with mom or dad at home. Homework can be anything from counting Cheerios to drawing pictures and keeping them in a folder. Make homework a positive ritual at home. When the real thing comes, it will not be a chore that takes away from playtime, but merely a challenging task. Staying involved with your child's homework will keep your connection strong.

please don't make me feel smaller than i am. it only makes me behave stupidly big.

When a parent scolds their child in front of their peer or another adult, the child feels embarrassed and possibly cringes, wanting to dig a hole and jump in it.

When the child has to act like a "big shot" it is to protect themselves. When you think about how they must feel when they are embarrassed because we shot them down, it is important to ask ourselves why at that moment was that necessary? *Who* was feeling insecure or embarrassed and then *who* paid the price for it? To scold a child in public is a knee jerk reaction to our own embarrassment. Does the child really take notice and learn at that moment? If at this point they are self-protecting by acting like a "big shot" the ship has sailed. It would be beneficial to avoid the misbehavior next time by addressing the matter when you are alone and have their full attention. A child will take much more notice if you talk quietly with them in private. Consider that next time the focus is on the behavior of the child, not the child and that as the parent you do need to help them correct it. Remember you are their greatest supporter, to embarrass and humiliate your child is a breach of the contract you made with yourself as a parent.

please don't be invisible at my school. it is my community and i need you as an ally.

It is very exciting for parents when they send their child off to nursery school and kindergarten and at the beginning they are very involved. It is during the later years that it is important to be connected to your child's school experience, ask your child what they are learning in school.

We do not all have fond memories of our school days, and our feelings may interfere or influence this. Maybe our reactions to authority, or peer pressure sour the curiosity of their experience. Does it bring back bad memories for you?

Sometimes going to our child's school causes us a flashback that results in inadequacy, fear or an unpleasant experience. It is important for our children to remain positive in their environment. Do not ridicule the teacher and cause a rivalry. It burdens the child with a loyalty bind.

Get to know the teachers, the administration, and the school community. It is your child's world outside of home. Their education is their vocation and having the right attitude about it will determine their career choices and lifestyle.

**please** don't make me feel that my mistakes are mortal sins. it upsets my sense of values.

News flash. Everybody makes mistakes. If a child is crucified for making mistakes then chances are they will refrain from taking risks. When their mistakes are made to feel like sins then their self-judgment effects their self-acceptance. As parents our job is to guide our children and provide them with the tools that will help them gain the experience they need to make sound decisions. From early childhood, children are making choices, everyday presents many decision-making opportunities. There will be good decisions and not so good. There is value in both.

With self-realization and understanding a child can grow up believing in themselves, learn from their mistakes, be willing to take more risks, and forgive themselves when necessary, recover and then move on. If not we have an individual who is like a deer frozen in the headlights stuck at the crossroads, sitting on the fence forever, never to be able to decide on anything. Rarely feeling good about the decisions they do make will create self-doubt. Commitment becomes a scary word because it takes follow through with persistence and the risk of making mistakes is too great. Help your child learn to take risks, and experience the fall, and finding a way to get up and try again!

**please** don't feed me fishsticks when you can very well teach me how to fish.

In today's world we are tempted by all of life's conveniences. We can take the path of least resistance in most everything. Our children are learning technology and faster ways of problem solving. As beneficial as this is to make production quicker and easier, they also lose the opportunity to witness the process of building something from scratch. It would be favorable and fun for your child to develop the patience to take on a project from beginning to end, to use their hands to build something with good old fashion tools.

**please** don't be soooo upset when i scream, "i hate you!". sometimes it isn't you i hate but your power to defeat me.

*"Sometimes?"* What is that suppose to mean? Unless you are a real ogre, or possessed by evil spirits, your child will not hate you. Why then do they despise us at these particular moments? Because, as parents we must set boundaries, and limits to ensure their safety and security. They are too young to process their feelings and find this difficult to admit. Admitting it means they need us. Therefore, they are placing themselves in a vulnerable position. Generally, no one likes to place himself or herself in a vulnerable position. And sometimes the idea that there is a big fat "No" that they can not get around can certainly deflate and challenge anyone.

On a positive note, when the child reacts with this feeling of hating you it confirms their understanding that you are the authority. However, the negative side to this is that if power is abused it will backfire. Too often parents say "no" for reasons that are not relative to the question at hand. When giving a "no" that warrants an explanation, then offer one. "No, because I said so" is not a fair or clear response. Remember they are watching us make decisions that in turn will teach them the process of decision-making.

**please** don't assign me to a role, it limits me to a predetermined legacy.

O.K. you, may have offered your son the position of Jr. Same as you in name only. Delightfully our children take on characteristics that remind us of Uncle Leo or ourselves or late Aunt Sylvia. The uncanny mannerisms and attitudes we see repeating themselves can also become a burden, a disguised version of another family member. Whether that family member is a pillar of society or a down and out drop out of society, by claiming our little Jimmy that he is just like your brother Joey can hinder the freedom of your child's own direction in life. When it becomes excessive in reminding your child that he is just like him or her, in looks, or attitude it is then planted in your child's head that their legacy has been predetermined, why then try to be someone other than THAT.

**please** don't tell me my fears are silly. they are terribly real and you can do much to reassure me if you try to understand.

When we laugh off their jitters, we are probably trying to minimize them or normalize them for their sake. It is an attempt to put them at ease, and our intentions are well meant. This is yet another opportunity to see the world from their perspective. When our child can not fall asleep and asks that we stay in the bedroom until they do, it is a difficult decision sometime for us. For one, we are eager to get a few minutes to ourselves or have adult time with our partner. And on the other hand our instincts tell us they are manipulating us to squeeze out yet more mommy/daddy and me time, and want attention. But what if they really are frightened, and do not want to be alone?

Remember, they are processing a lot of information and laying down in their bed for the first time after having had a whirlwind day of instruction, play, relational negotiation, media, external stimuli and all the rest, they are now by themselves in the night…alone processing all of it. You can test this by asking them how their day was when they get home from school. Many times you will get a vague answer because they themselves do not know, they have not yet processed their day. But, at bedtime this is why they may feel frightened. They are asking us to understand that their experiences are overwhelming as much as they are new and exciting.

**please** don't take too much notice of my small afflictions. sometimes they get me the attention i need.

When your child sniffles, or cries give them the attention they need. Children are not always as carefree as we would like to believe. So when it is apparent that they are searching for some attention from you, offer your time, your touch. If your child likes to talk, be a good listener. You will come to recognize their method or the non-verbal cues that indicate they can use an embrace. Whichever way you have learned to understand your child. Sometimes just a hug for no reason or "you're a great kid" goes a long way and they feel better and loved, which can put them back on track.

**please** don't allow me to speak to you disrespectfully. you are the example of how i will relate
to others in my world.

Parents do not set out to be parents expecting their children will "talk back," "sass them", "give them lip" and be down right disrespectful and rude. Most of us learned growing up that this behavior would land us in a heap of trouble. So, how does it happen? The difference today in parenting, opposed to back in yesteryear, is that parents are taking the incorrect and unhealthy approach that their child can be their peer. By setting boundaries from the beginning, will create a clear distinction between parent and child. If your child yells at you or makes an inappropriate demand, right then and there it is important for them to know that this behavior will never be tolerated. Explain why, because you are the parent and they are the child and it is unacceptable in this relationship and any relationship. Remember that it is by nature that we test boundaries and rules. Children are very good at it.

**please** don't make me relive your painful childhood memories.

Unfortunately no one has had a completely perfect childhood experience. And what we take away from our childhood can be pain, deep wounds, and distortions. When parenting our children we can be triggered back to a time when we were hurt, and misunderstood or worse neglected and abused. It is important to be aware of separating those memories and putting them into their rightful place, the past. It is easy to slip and displace some of those hurts on to the rearing of our own children. Make sure, you take time for self-reflection. A good therapist can help you resolve those early traumas privately. Like ghosts they can rear their scary heads and haunt us. Our children were not there no need to introduce them to the skeletons in our closet.

please don't buy me ice cream.

When a child is feeling a powerful emotion it can cause parents a discomfort. It may be difficult to know how to comfort a child, who is grieving, or feeling rejected, or just having a bad day and feeling insecure. Children do not always need us to resolve their problems or buy them something to make them feel better. But they do need us to allow them to ride the wave of that emotion. Allowing them to feel their feelings will enable them to develop self-discovery skills. Feeling our emotions help us get in touch with who we really are. In turn this develops a deeper meaningful human experience for all of us as it teaches us compassion for ourselves as well as others.

**please** don't nag. if you do, i shall have to protect myself by ignoring you.

Choose your battles. It is so tempting to constantly remind our children to clean their room, do their chores, do their homework, brush their teeth, pick up their socks, take out the garbage, walk the dog... There are a million things for them to do and we must make sure they do each and every one of them, we have to make them responsible adults... HALT! Unfortunately, after the first or second request, the rest of the list sounds like waw waw waw waw waw waw to them.

Yes, it is important for us as parents to guide our children into a world of order and cleanliness. We are afraid that if we do not teach them now, they will one day have their own home and live on a heap of dirty laundry and pizza boxes, and then where will we sit when we want to visit with them? And what guilt we will feel because we never nagged them enough to learn how to pick up after themselves. But what we really want is for our children to value a clean home, and an orderly way to live.

We want to impress upon them that a chaotic home can be a distraction to a productive and successful life. Communicating, rather then battling or nagging will be more effective in explaining to them that the home is a place of pride, it is a reflection of how we see ourselves, as well as our respect for other family members. You want them to hear that they are part of this family and we work together to keep a nice home.

**please** don't put me off when i ask questions.
if you do, i will stop asking and seek
information elsewhere.

How many times did we as children want to ask our parent to explain something that did not make sense? Questions such as how does the radio announcer fit into that tiny little radio... is there life on other planets?

What a compliment to be approached and expected to know the answer or at least be the one who will take the time to research it with them. When we ask a question, it usually means we are seeking for truths. We ask the person we trust to give us an honest answer. Our children ask us because they trust us. Granted, questions get thrown at us during inopportune times, or when we are preoccupied with our own questions about our own concerns. But if we are to raise curious minds and nurture them in a way that will encourage them to always seek the truth do we not want to be on the forefront. Besides, if they seek their information elsewhere who knows what they will be told? It is our job to encourage our children to ask questions in order to expand their mind. It is how we respond to their quest that in the long run will develop their confidence to broaden the arena and seek reliable sources.

**please** don't be inconsistent with your promises. that completely confuses me and makes me lose faith in you.

Is your child asking you to remain in the same good mood each and every day? I hope not. But they are asking you to remain sure and steady like a strong ship in a turbulent sea. They are asking for you to ride the storm during the unpredictable chaos and stressful moments by maintaining a sense of calm and control. Their request also implies the belief of "say what you mean and mean what you say". Be reliable. Your child will come across many individuals who renege on their promises, cancel at the last minute, or fail to show up at all, both literally and figuratively. Be the one your child can count on, the one who has developed an understanding of them through experience and time spent together. When your child comes to understand what you stand for and what you believe in, they are on solid ground with you. Parents provide security by being consistent. Like that old comfortable sweatshirt that feels so good and is worn into the shape that fits just right. Be their "old sweatshirt". They grow so fast they will never fit into a sweatshirt long enough for it to get old. Be consistent in your love, attention, and character, be for the most part predictable in your response to them.

**please** don't forget that i can't thrive
without lots of love and understanding.
but i don't need to tell you. do i?

It is not enough to love and understand them. It is enough when they know it.

So tell them and show them every chance you get. They eventually move away so now is your chance!

**please** don't share all of your personal problems with me. i should not have to worry about you or take care of you.

No child has had the type of experiences an adult encounters in their short lives and must never be asked to deal with adult problems. They are <u>not</u> adults. They have not experienced problem solving, outside of their small world experiences. When parents burden their children with their own worries, the result is a child feeling over-protective and anxious. This will place strain on them and cause unnecessary anxiety. This will interrupt their schoolwork, social life, and cause them to grow up too fast.

Seek counsel or confide in an adult friend when troubles become too difficult to handle alone. If your child detects there is a problem, reassure them that they do not have to help you solve it. That is your job.

**please** don't ever suggest that you are perfect or infallible it gives me too great a shock when
i discover that you are not.

OOH! The verdict is in... you are a HUMAN. And everybody knows it, including your children. This is not to say that they need to know about the dark side of you and the reckless behavior in your younger days. But it is important for them to know you made mistakes and will continue to make mistakes. Placing yourself up on a pedestal will only put you in a precarious situation when you come crashing to the ground. Do not be so full of yourself that being HUMAN is a bad thing. Your child will learn from you about how to recover from mistakes and poor decisions that are inevitable and yet a valuable fact of life.

**please** don't ever think that it is beneath you to apologize to me. an honest apology makes me feel wonderfully warm towards you.

What we nurture are relationships. Relationships never work when they are one sided. Do not make excuses when you have made a mistake, or happen to be shortsighted on a matter, or lost your temper. Instead, apologize. Be accountable for your actions. You are modeling responsible and mature emotional behavior. When a parent is able to communicate a sincere apology the child in turn feels loved and regarded.

If they can experience an adult whom they love and respect initiating responsibility for their foibles, they too will learn to take responsibilities for their own. This avoids a lifetime of playing that no win contest of the "blame game".

please don't assume i am a smaller version of you. i am me.

How many times do we look at our children and are reminded of ourselves? This triggers memories of our own past. They begin to influence the way we see our children's future. It can take the form of fear, disappointments, misjudgments and such. It is our job to protect them from harmful circumstances, however, to shield them because we want to avoid regrets will not allow them to experience a multiple perspective.

Guiding and directing their lives in the way we wanted ours to turn out will not make up for anything lost. Times are different, their parents are different, and they are different. Celebrate the unique qualities of your child.

**please** don't bicker with my other parent in
front of me.
it confuses the meaning of power.

It is normal for two adults who are married or living together to argue from time to time. Explain to your child that two adults can see things differently and a respectful debate is healthy. It is important that your child recognize the freedom of speech demonstrated in their own household. As a rule no parent should dominate over the other causing an unbalanced distribution of power. If a child detects that one parent is bullying the other, then they learn to either bully others out of fear of being a victim. Or choose to be the victim. Either way, they lose and internalize a disregard for others or themselves.

**please** don't forget i love to experiment. i can't develop without it. so please put up with me.

Do you really want your child to wait until they are off your radar to experiment with whatever is introduced to them? Why not while toddling around encourage them to play in a tub of spaghetti, or when old enough, cook up some concoction for dinner. Not only does it stimulate their tactile and creative impulses, it allows them a freedom that eventually they may not have time nor an interest in once they discover the concrete world. But early experimentation, whether it gets lost or put on hold, will remain in their spirit and memory. It will inspire them to push the envelope and be more creative than their peers who were forbidden to take that leap, or heard messages like, " Look at this mess!" or "you're ruining your good clothes". You have the opportunity to teach them cause and effect that will come in handy when they are compelled to experiment with more dangerous matter. It is important to know that discouraging a child to experiment and responding with the fear that things might get out of control if you loosen the reins will only backfire later. Be there to support your child in their early days to encourage their innate desire to experiment.

**please** don't gossip in front of me it makes me question your sincerity.

There is a term known as "two faced". Unless, we are able to speak face to face with those we pass judgements on, we know that it is a negative display to gossip about them behind their backs. It is confusing to our children when they witness this act. Concluding in their minds that either their parents are cowards who can not be honest with people they know or their sincerity is phony when they are friendly to that same person.

This then compromises their trust in us.

please don't protect me from life's disappointments. i can only learn the hard knocks by experience.

It is so heart wrenching to see our children sad over life's disappointments and injustices. But as we have come to learn the truth, that is life. During these sad times, hug them show them how much you love them and be supportive, acknowledge their heartbreak and give them the room to process it, the way they need to. Just sitting with them quietly is all they need, just knowing you are there holding their hand.

**please** don't praise me for every little accomplishment it results in a false sense of security.

As babies and toddlers and all children reach milestones and we praise them in ceremonious glory. These early accomplishments are many times by human design. When we praise our children for completing a task or figuring out how to use the telephone we are overdoing it. Although it is important for them to know you are proud of them, however too much on basic tasks are sending a message that their ability was in question to begin with.

If the focus is about you feeling proud shift it to how are they feeling about themselves, are they proud? Are they performing for your approval or have they raised the bar higher for their own personal goals and satisfaction.

**please** don't find fault with my friends in order to make me feel more superior to them.

It is with good intentions, to boost your child's self-esteem. But sometimes parents can unfairly compare other children to their own by finding fault. As a result this impacts your child's feelings toward those they regard as their friends, perhaps doubting what it is about them they find special. Better to build up their friends with noted praise and compliments that in turn justifies the reason your child enjoys spending time with them in the first place.

**please** don't forget how quickly i am growing up. it must be very exhausting for you to keep up with me. but do try.

Raising children is exhausting to say the least. The military recruiters claim the army is "the hardest job you'll ever love". Well, they may not have had kids. Raising children is a job, the perk is that we love them and are amazed by them. At the same time, the exhaustion of rearing them, listening to them, shuffling them to and fro, cooking, cleaning, shopping, teaching, worrying, and the list goes on can not only create physical exhaustion but mental exhaustion and emotional exhaustion. It may take until they turn five or six and go off to school before you are able to formulate a complete sentence in your head. Maybe not until they are age 12 can you get a decent night sleep only to be up nights waiting for them to come home a few years later. It is a full time job with no vacation time, no pension, and no retirement. Do they even understand that? No, not until they are parents themselves.

Until then it is so important for you to take care of yourself. Burn out and depression are very real, therefore do not tempt it and exhaust yourself by being the champion caretaker.

Children deserve a childhood. The more rested and informed you are the better for their growth and development.

please don't forget that i cannot explain myself as well as i would like. that is why i am not always clear.

In our daily lives many of us work with other adults, it is an adjustment to shift gears in conversing with our young children. It is not always apparent that they are frustrated with trying to explain what it is they want. Sometimes they get the sequence of a story wrong, or drone on about some trivial dialogue they had with their friend in the school cafeteria that one would need to have "been there" to appreciate. But alas, our children are working out and practicing unbeknownst to them the art of conversation, the monologue, the performance of public speaking and should have our undivided attention.

There is a time and place to correct their pronunciation and grammar but not while they are delivering their riveting soliloquy. Now is the time to enjoy their presence, their pleasure in sharing with you, as their special invited guest as they delve into their intricate and wonderful world in the way they experience it. Watch them with your eyes wide open and with a smile on your face that says, if you could you would pay top dollar for another front row seat.

and...**please** keep yourself healthy and fit. i
need you.

As busy as you are, remember to make a medical appointment for yourself, get the annual check up. Have your eyes checked. Conquer the fear and go, if not for you for them. Get some exercise, you are a role model, and they learn how to be healthy from you. And as long as you are fit, you should have an easier time meeting their needs.

Get healthy and stay well.

Having a family when planned and prepared is a wonderful celebration of life.

# After thoughts

There are many challenges to raising a child. Our responsibility as parents is to nurture our children in ways that help them develop into confident, loving, caring people who in turn will make contributions to the next generation and to society.

Obviously it is not easy to parent and making important decisions should take careful planning.

My second daughter is very different in personality than my first daughter, which meant I needed to start all over again in my approach to our relationship. One size does not fit all, and needing to be fair to her meant I now needed to make adjustments. Family life is a constant adjustment, so be flexible when you can.

How your child comes into your life, whether it is planned, or a surprise, adopted, or fostered, remember this opportunity is a gift. And everyday this gift can bring joy and fulfillment.